**HANDS-ON HELP FOR MAKING
THE MOST OF YOUR RELATIONSHIP
WITH YOUR HORSE**

Dr. Mike's Horsemanship Horse Owner's Modern Keys for Success

MICHAEL GUERINI, PhD

Dr. Mike's Horsemanship Horse Owner's Modern Keys for Success
A book in the Dr. Mike's Horsemanship Guide series

Copyright © 2013 by Michael Guerini. All rights reserved.

To subscribe to receive our newsletter and periodic updates, as well as a free gift of five (5) additional Riding Exercises, please send an email to the following address and put "subscribe" in the subject line:

newsletter@dunmovinranch.com

To visit the Dun Movin Ranch website, type the following address into your web browser or scan the QR code with your smartphone or webcam:

www.dunmovinranch.com

Set in Times New Roman

ISBN-13: 978-1497311169
ISBN-10: 1497311160

Cover and interior design by Ken J. Howe © 2014

Horse Owner's Modern Keys for Success

Dedication

To all the horses and riders —
Thank you for allowing me to be a part of your experience.
May you all learn to communicate as a team, ride safer,
and have more fun.

About the Author

Michael Guerini (Dr. Mike) is a horseman, author, and scientist from Gilroy, California. From an early age, he gained valuable experience working with his family to train horses. To this day, he continues to work with his family to develop a whole horse relationship training and education program. Michael studies Dressage, performance horses and teaches routinely on the merits of good horsemanship and improving the relationship of the horse and rider.

www.dunmovinranch.com

In 2011, Michael introduced his first work of fiction about a scientist who becomes a veterinarian and puts all his skills to work in solving medical problems in animals (*Old Towne: Beginnings*) followed in 2012 by his first work of poetry (*Of Horses & Life*). Michael is a Lifetime member of the American Quarter Horse Association. With his unique blend of ground work, dressage, and general colt starting philosophy, he can help you build a stronger relationship with your horse.

Michael is also the co-inventor of the **Equine Hydro-T**, a water-saving, pulsating nozzle attachment for equine physical therapy and oral hygiene. To find out more about this innovative product, its uses and availability, please visit **www.hydrot.com** or scan this QR code with your smart phone or webcam:

Acknowledgments

Barbara Guerini is a horsewoman, competitive dog handler, wife, and mother from Gilroy, California. Barbara, Mom to Dr. Mike, is a wonderful teacher full of patience and wisdom. She and Dr. Mike work horses together and discuss all aspects of training, confirmation, and showing. Whenever something puzzles Dr. Mike, he stops in and seeks counsel from Mom.

Horse Owner's Modern Keys for Success

Throughout our life, we continue to grow and develop by learning new concepts, ideas, and ways of succeeding. Our life with horses is no different. From the first day that I sat on the back of a horse I started to learn... learn from the horse. The horse, when we listen, is a most excellent teacher. Complementing the lessons from our horses with information from professionals, mentors, coaches, and friends helps us to grow as horsemen and horsewomen. This collection of works comes from much of what I have learned from many horses and colleagues. Added to my knowledge is that of my mentor and coach — Barbara Guerini, my mother.

I set out to create a book that summarizes many of the thoughts and ideas that I embrace when coaching people to ride or that I teach in my horsemanship clinics.

Thank you for taking the time to purchase and read this book.

CONTENTS

CHAPTER 1

Essays on Horsemanship

The 6 C's of Horsemanship: Building Blocks for Success in Relationship Training

Many of us benefit from Natural Horsemanship and Foundation Training methods. We dive into books, watch videos, attend seminars and go to clinics to learn all we can to develop a strong emotional, mental and physical foundation in all of our horses. These methods use a "building block" approach to help us focus on assembling a good horse that is willing and able to perform. In this approach to training each lesson needs to be learned and firmly in place before we can teach the next lesson.

I believe very few people are born great horsemen and women, the majority of us work all our lives to become better horsemen and women. As I work to become a better horseman, I have had to step back and look at my own "building blocks." The 6 C's of Horsemanship are the Building Blocks for Success that I teach at my clinics and use in my own barn.

THE SIX C's OF HORSEMANSHIP

The **6 C's of Horsemanship** are "building blocks" for having <u>Confidence</u>, keeping <u>Control</u>, maintaining <u>Consistency</u>, riding with <u>Collection</u>, having <u>Compassion</u> and keeping an attitude of <u>Calmness</u>. Together these ideas help us build a lasting relationship with our horse.

- **Compassion**
- **Control**
- **Collection**
- **Confidence**
- **Calmness**
- **Consistency**

So how do we use the 6 C's of Horsemanship to gain success in the saddle?

CONFIDENCE

When we ride, we want to be confident in our riding skills and our horse. To gain <u>confidence</u> we practice, learn from others, go to clinics and we take small steps. If I wanted to ride on a 5-day trail ride, I would first build up my confidence and my horse's confidence by taking a 1-day ride.

CONTROL

In order for us to gain confidence, we need to learn to <u>control</u> our horse and the space around our horse.

CONSISTENCY

To build confidence and establish control we need to practice with consistency. As a rider, it is our obligation to be consistent in our training and riding methods. When we are consistent, have a plan, and follow our plan we build confidence in our horse and our abilities.

COLLECTION

To maintain control we need to keep our bodies and our horse's body collected. We cannot expect control when our arms are waving all around and our horses are racing through open fields. Maintaining collection of our body, our speed and the horse's flexibility helps us to be confident and in control.

COMPASSION and CALMNESS

As we teach our horse, we need to remember to have compassion. When I go out on a trail ride I want to enjoy time with my horse and I want to enjoy the scenery and most of all I want this to be full of calmness.

As we embark on the day and each time we go to the barn remember — our horse should be just as calm at the end of our ride as he was when he was standing in his stall.

I am certain that the **6 C's of Horsemanship** will be a valuable tool for building knowledge and in turn realizing results as you work with your horses.

Common Sense and Horsemanship

As I was growing up the Western movies were becoming rare genres. The classics and some of the newer horse movies were fun to watch especially when the horseman rode his trusty horse over hills, through herds of cattle and even down the side of a cliff. At night, I would lay my head down, think of those rides, and wish for a day when I could ride my horse just like the rider in the movie.

My mother asked me what I found so thrilling about the idea of riding my horse down the side of a cliff. I smiled at her and said because then I would be a great rider.

Thankfully, for the sake and safety of my horse, I never made that ride… instead; I chose to follow the path of learning how to be a great horseman.

As I work with many horses and learn from some of the great horsemen and horsewomen, I realize that good horsemanship and common sense go together.

Common sense is doing what is prudent and using good judgment. Why when we hear someone describe how and where he or she rode a horse this past weekend do we cringe?

As the rider is describing his ride we never envision the great western rides in the movies… we envision wrecks, injuries or at the very least a scrape or two. We often walk away wondering if this rider has any common sense!

All too often people use the image of riding a horse in a movie as the goal of their training program. People forget that the horse in the movie has been trained and worked with consistently in order to achieve the result we see on the big screen.

Unfortunately, common sense seems to be missing from many riders.

Great riders can sit on a horse and navigate obstacles.

Great riders have excellent balance and good hand and eye coordination.

Great riders feel free and unworried as they ride.

Great riders do not always use common sense when riding.

Great horsemen can do everything that a great rider can do AND they use common sense. They first teach the horse how to work off leg pressure and respond to a cue.

Great horsemen listen to the horse's body language and then adapt the training program so that they are as compassionate as possible yet remain in control and offer consistent instruction to the horse.

Many people who ride want to make a connection with the horse; they want to build a relationship. Thank goodness we have many excellent horsemen and women who demonstrate techniques and methods for helping us build this relationship. Sadly though these learned horsemen and horsewomen cannot teach us common sense.

How do we incorporate common sense into our riding and training programs?

First, we need to stop and decide what realistic goals we want to achieve. Then we need to develop an approach that relies on safety, knowledge, and good judgment.

Take the time to make informed decisions, take the time to learn how to ride correctly, take the time to learn about the horse you ride. As a horse owner, we all get to decide if we want to be a great rider or a great horseman.

I hope we can take the time to become great horsemen and horsewomen.

From the Ground Up: Maintaining your Horse's Foundation Training

Over the past 10 years, we have heard a great deal about "Foundation Training" programs for horses. Simply put, a foundation-training program is about training our horse physically, mentally and emotionally by using ground work and saddle work.

Physically we teach our horse to be able to walk forward, backward, and move hips and shoulders with the least amount of contact by the rider. The mental aspect occurs when we gain our horse's attention. The emotional part of the training comes when we lessen the impact of the horse's fight or flight instinct.

Foundation training is not a "hurry-up" training program. Similar to construction where a strong foundation is needed before walls are built, we ensure our horse learns lesson 1 before proceeding to lesson 2.

How is it that many horses having been trained seem to "forget" lessons they have learned? The answer is simple:

We forget to perform maintenance on our horse.

We all know that maintenance can help us avoid costly repairs and extend the life expectancy of many of the things we own. Our car, for example, performs better with routine care. Homeowners know that preventative maintenance, although it seems expensive and time consuming initially, is far more cost effective than using a crisis management approach of scrambling when something is in need of repair.

Just as with our home or car, our horse continually needs maintenance. Without it, we find ourselves wondering what went wrong with our horse. We say things like, "My horse used to lope for me," or "My horse used to load in the trailer," and "So why won't he make smooth lead changes now?"

How do we retain our horse's foundation? We consistently review and then, if necessary, reestablish the previous lessons.

In order to maintain my foundation training I begin each ride by reminding my horse of the basics. I make sure my horse walks forward, backward and moves her hip and shoulders. I do this on the ground and then in the saddle. In less than five minutes, I know if my horse's foundation of knowledge is in good shape for the ride or the lesson I have planned. If not, I go back to a review of the basics until my horse does these things correctly.

Why do I go through all of this? Without this check-up, my horse sometimes seems ill prepared for a new lesson.

You might think that your horse is fully trained and you are simply riding for fun and are not trying to teach your horse new things. Good for you! Still, you need to perform maintenance to keep you horse well prepared for everything you will ask him to do.

So, if you encounter a time where your horse seems to have forgotten something he should know, before you blame your horse, please stop and ask yourself—have I been doing my maintenance? I am sure your horse will appreciate the upkeep.

Conditioned Response Training:
"Pressure and Release"

Recently I was asked this question by a lady at one of my clinics. "What is "Pressure and Release" and is it something that will make my horse better?" When horse people talk about "Pressure and Release" they are talking about touching a horse in a certain spot then getting a specific response. This is called a conditioned response.

The basic idea behind a conditioned response is that when step A happens, if properly trained, step B will happen next. Horses are sensitive animals. A slight bit of pressure (either in the form of a touch, a yell, a wave of the hand) can be enough to get the horse to move away. We can use this to our advantage by using "Pressure and Release" training. In "Pressure and Release" training I work with my horse so he understands that when I apply pressure to a specific part of his body he responds by moving away from that pressure. As long as the rider uses the smallest amount of pressure and the horse responds correctly this as a good thing. For example, touching a horse on the left shoulder means the horse needs to move his shoulders to the right.

One of the important things to remember while using "Pressure and Release" is that our entire body and the way we ride effects how good of a response we get from our horse. We need to actively guide the horse with our body movements. In the example above where I am moving the shoulders to the right I also need to be looking to the right and using my hands to help guide my horse to the right. I place pressure where I want the horse to move away from and I make sure to guide him with my eyes, upper body and gently with my hands towards the opening (non pressure place).

"Pressure and Release" requires that I immediately take away the pressure once my horse begins to respond. Only by riding with my hands, legs, and body does the horse understand that a touch on the left shoulder means move shoulders to the right. So you see, "Pressure and Release" is about actively riding and communicating with your horse.

One part of this process that is very important to remember is that we need to give the horse an opening to move towards. The opening is the place where there is no pressure. The horse will recognize this as the place we want him to go because there is nothing blocking his way to get there. Without this opening the horse has nowhere to go and will become frustrated or confused. We as the rider need to make sure that when we ask the horse to do something, we give him clear directions (Pressure), the place to go (Opening), and the reward (Release).

Let us also remember that "Pressure and Release" works on the Ground as well. We use the same ideas of touch and body language to get the horse to move in a direction we choose when we are doing our ground work. So if we train with the idea of being an active rider and using our hands and legs and body we will succeed with "Pressure and Release." We can be confident that we can move our horse away from danger because he responds to "Pressure and Release."

I hope that you can see the benefit to training with "Pressure and Release" and how using this will make your horse more responsive to you as a rider.

CHAPTER 2

Reminders for Success
with Horses

Horse Training & Relationship-Building Reminders

Build a foundation with each horse. This foundation is centered on respect of horse for rider and rider for horse, ability of the horse to accept leadership from the rider/handler, movement of all body parts of the horse with the lightest possible aide/cue by the rider/handler. Then work towards the goals you have for yourself and the horse. As you specialize, your training will be different but the foundation should be the same for all.

What follows is a collection of sayings, ideas, and thoughts that can help you improve your horsemanship and relationship with your horse. The ideas presented in this section are meant as guides and reminders for all that you must do to build that strong foundation and relationship with your horse.

This work is divided into three subsections with 15 ideas in each section. There are many more ideas but these are the most common shared thoughts between Dr. Mike and Barbara.

<u>Subsections</u>

General thoughts for successful horsemanship.

Working with your horse on the ground.

Working with your horse in the saddle.

General Thoughts
for Successful Horsemanship

1) Safety of the rider/handler and the horse must be the number one priority.

2) Wear appropriate clothing: close toed, sturdy shoes, long pants, and protective shirt when working with horses.

3) Get off your cell phone or earbuds/radio and minimize distractions.

4) Do not try to train your dog at the same time as the horse, choose one or the other, they both require different training methods.

5) Do not go out to the barn looking for a fight with your horse, if you look for a fight you will find one.

6) Watch how your horse interacts with his/her settings. Look at your horse at play or just moving about in the stall, paddock, or pasture. You will learn what your horse can do by just watching.

7) Clean and mend your equipment regularly for both use and safety needs.

8) Training, conformation, warm-up exercises, and number of repetitive actions, rider balance, arena footing, hoof care, health care, and nutrition are all important.

9) Do not chase your horse; teach the horse to come when called.

10) If you are not having success with your horse, stop and think a moment before you decide on your next plan of action.

11) Keep your emotions in check when working with horses, they can sense emotion and the fight or flight mechanism they live by can take control of the situation.

12) Know your surroundings and be able to keep your horse safe from debris or items that can hurt your horse and thereby you.

13) Make sure your horse goes forwards, backwards and moves side to side.

14) Whoa means whoa...when you ask for it make sure it happens.

15) Reward the positive behavior and put your horse to work moving his/her feet when negative behaviors happen.

NOTES

Working with your horse on the ground

1) Work both sides of your horse.

2) Ground work is the key to a foundation of good riding.

3) Two hands on the lead shank (if you want the horse to move forward have your hand open/palm facing the direction of travel; if you want your horse to slow down or stop, have your hand closed around the rope with the palm facing the rear of the horse.

4) Teach the go forward cue (good for spooky situations, leaving a stall and trailer loading).

5) Change of direction exercises help you and your horse get soft and work as a team.

6) Teach a horse to respect your space (it is not a lap dog).

7) In the round pen, an inside turn is worth 500 points more than an outside turn and shows respect.

8) Warming up your horse needs to include lateral work, do not just go around in circles, engage the mind of your horse.

9) Quit jerking on the lead shank all the time when you are doing something with your horse. The horse decides it is unenjoyable and then you begin to have problems.

10) Lunging is not the solution to all problems.

12) Control of your horse's speed/footfalls on the ground will lead to success in the saddle.

13) Stay aware and alert for your protection and that of your horse. When leading your horse, make sure his/her head is next to your shoulder.

14) The ground is a place to build a lasting relationship with the horse.

15) The best time to de-sensitize your horse to new items is when you are working him/her on the ground.

NOTES

Working with your horse in the saddle

1) Wearing a helmet is a great idea (safety) when riding.

2) Use pre-signals (shoulders, seat, and eyes) and know how an aide and a pre-signal are different.

3) Keep your eyes up when riding.

4) Master the exercise at the walk before going to the trot and trot before cantering.

5) Know how to ride with your driving and bending aides and aide of opposition (outside rein).

6) Knowing and feeling the footfalls of your horse will allow you to use the proper aide at the correct time and get the right result with the least amount of effort.

7) Centered riding helps you maintain balance and feel on the horse.

8) Make your horse stand still when you mount and do so from both sides of the horse.

9) Better to dismount if you are fearful of a situation than to stay on the back of your horse and get hurt (you or the horse).

10) Do not ride the same exercise repetitively. Injuries can occur with repetitive motions. Alternate exercises to reduce repetitive injury risks.

11) Learn where your seat bones are located so that you can use them.

12) Use a mounting block if you are not so flexible as to leg up. There is no shame in this -- only care for your horse and yourself. Also good for horses who often have chiropractic issues.

13) Know how to do the one rein emergency stop.

14) Use many exercises and movements of your horse to engage his/her brain.

15) Move all body parts of the horse with the slightest amount of aide.

NOTES

CHAPTER 3

Essays on the Horse Owner to Horse Professional Relationship

The Horse Owner – Horse Trainer Relationship

This is the first in a series of essays on how we as owners interact with the different professionals that we rely on in the horse world. Some of these interactions include:

Horse Owner – Horse Trainer

Rider – Riding Instructor

Horse Owner – Clinician

Horse Owner – Veterinarian and Farrier

Horse Owner – Stable/arena owner/manager

The horse owner – horse trainer relationship is very important for developing a horse. As a horse owner, I have worked with quite a few trainers in the past to have my horses started and developed. As a trainer, I have the privilege of working with a number of horses in my training program.

At times, I hear fellow trainers express sadness that they have an unhappy client (horse owner) and other times I hear of an owner who is not happy with the trainer. I lend an ear when people want to talk and along the way, I have learned some important things that I practice as an owner and a trainer. Here I share some thoughts to help you with this process.

1) Research trainers and find out what they have to offer you as a horse owner.

When I say research, I mean look them up online, ask for references from the trainer, check out their record in the discipline of your interest, make an appointment and ask to speak with him or her for 15 minutes about training philosophy and ask that you get to see the training arena, feed, and stables. If you like your horse to have supplements, find out if the facility will give your horse supplements. Check out some videos he or she might have available. Find out how much training/riding is done by the trainer verses others on staff.

2) Begin the relationship with communication.

This is equally important for both the trainer and the owner.

As the owner, you will want to share with the trainer what your goals are for the horse. If you have done your homework as suggested in #1 above, you will know that this trainer and you are compatible. Be prepared to write these down as part of the contract process.

As the trainer, you want to be clear in sharing your philosophy and how you will develop this horse. You want to share a plan for the first 30 days that includes you calling or emailing the owner with some updates. Updates need to be more than "the horse is nice." As the trainer, sit down and give some pluses and minuses and an honest evaluation.

Set up a review of the horse's progress on a routine basis. For this, I suggest every 30 or 45 days needs a face-to-face meeting or detailed phone conversation. You may learn that your horse is not suited for a particular discipline…so listen to the trainer. As an owner, listen to what the trainer is saying about the horse. We all think our horse's are amazing, but just like us they have some faults.

3) Begin the relationship with a written contract.

Any owner or trainer who does not want to start the relationship with a written contract is not doing things correctly. Make sure the contract has a release of liability, terms of payment, what fees will be due for relevant services (veterinarian, farrier, etc), understanding of when the owner can stop by (what are the business hours), how much riding lesson time is included so that the owner learns how to ride the horse (if that is part of the owner's goals). Many things go into a written contract and you must remember this is a business arrangement, so start the process off correctly.

4) Have a Veterinarian check your horse before starting training.

Both the trainer and the owner have a stake in making certain the horse going into training is sound. For young horses, make sure the growth plates in the knees are closed. For all horses, make sure they are up to date on vaccinations, worming, farrier work, and that the horse is sound (basic flexion tests, radiographs if indicated). Trainers and owners alike do not like to learn a horse is lame after the first ride. This is not good for anyone.

5) See and show the horse in action.

As the owner, you need to make sure you take an interest in the progress of the horse. Take some time to see the horse ridden or shown. As the trainer, make opportunities available for the owner to see the horse in action.

I am sure you can come up with other items of importance in the horse-owner/horse-trainer relationship and I look forward to you sharing your thoughts.

Following paragraph contributed by Trainer Bethe Mounce of American Romance Equestrian.

americanromanceequestrian.com

Owner must realize that trainer has other horses to ride/train and theirs is not the only one in the herd. And owner must realize trainer is human....and has another life outside of horses, now and then that other life has to take priority. Trainers get sick, horses get sick, owners get sick...stuff happens! Owners must realize that the horses' health and welfare comes first. Owners must realize that the internet is not the place to go searching for answers. Owners must realize that the horse they bought may or may not be suited for them. A cheap horse often means thousands in training. And for those trainers who ride the young ones, there is NO clock. And owners must realize that chit chatting to rider while rider is on horse can often mean a trip to the ER by rider. Trainer/rider will talk afterwards, unfocused trainers have accidents. And please don't bring your kids to run around like hellions at the barn! And your dogs too. A barn is full of accidents waiting to happen, never a question of if, but when.

— *Bethe Mounce*, 2013

The Rider – Riding Instructor Relationship

This is the second in a series of essays on how we as owners interact with the different professionals that we rely on in the horse world. Some of these interactions include:

The horse owner – horse trainer relationship was discussed in the last essay. This time we are looking to the Rider – Riding Instructor relationship and things you can do to help this interaction be a success. Here are a few items to think about.

Riders:

1) Keep to the schedule

If you have a scheduled riding lesson, be on time or try to cancel at least 24 hours in advance. Yes, emergencies happen but if the instructor has reserved a spot for you, he/she might be able to fill the spot with another student if you must cancel.

2) Have your tack ready

If you have a piece of tack that you know needs repair or cleaning before the next lesson, take the time to do that before the start of the riding lesson.

3) Have your horse ready

If you are riding your own horse, have your horse tacked up and ready to ride/work with at the designated start time for your lesson.

4) Put your cell phone away (and not in your pant pocket)

In the world, we rely on our phone for many things but during the lesson, we need to pay attention to both the horse and instructor. Most lessons are an hour at the most and it is reasonable that you can go without a phone for at least 60 minutes. Most lesson providers understand if there is a pressing issue that may need your attention (sick family member, work issue) but you must ask yourself — can you really be at your best for the lesson and the horse if a pressing issue distracts you.

This is also an issue of safety. If you are not paying attention, you will have a time when you get hurt.

5) Do your homework and be prepared

If your instructor gave you some homework, try to do that in between lessons or at least be honest and tell him/her that you did not do your homework. Instructors can help you best if they know what you have been doing.

6) Leave as many distractions at home/car as possible (children, dogs, etc)

For your lesson, it is a good idea if you can minimize the number of distractions during your lesson time. When you cannot pay full attention to the lesson, you and your horse are not optimally prepared for learning. Again, there are safety considerations here. Distractions can keep you from focusing on the task and this leads to a situation where you or the horse can get hurt.

7) Share goals with your instructor

Make sure you take the time to email or communicate with the riding instructor what your goals are and ask him/her to let you know how he/she will help you with your goals. Every instructor should be able to help you grow as a rider and should push you to excel and you need to accept or discuss with them how much they might be pushing you. However, make sure the instructor is ready to help you with your goals.

Riding Instructor:

1) Keep to the schedule

As an instructor it is important that you remain on schedule, are at the arena at the designated lesson time and that you keep the lesson on track. Sure, horses and students may take a bit longer but it is bad form for the instructor to not be at the arena for the start time.

2) Put your cell phone away

Pay attention to the student. This is an issue of safety, liability, and responsibility and if you wish for the student to pay attention to you, then you must give them your attention.

3) Have a plan for the lesson

It is the instructor's responsibility to have a plan and communicate the lesson plan to the student. By having a plan, it shows a commitment to the education process.

4) Have your arena prepared

Have a safe and groomed (dirt/sand prepared) area to work with the horse and rider safely.

5) Leave as many distractions at the barn as possible

Just as the rider needs to leave distractions out and away from the arena, the instructor needs to do the same thing.

6) Listen to the student's goals but push them to improve

The instructor needs to show the student how the lesson is helping him/her get to the goals. At the same time, push the student to go further, develop more, and challenge him/herself as a rider.

If the rider and riding instructor follow these steps, it leads to a more conducive and safe learning environment. Build this relationship by communicating, setting goals, and being prepared.

As in all my essays, these are items for you to consider. I am sure you can come up with other items of importance in this relationship and I look forward to you sharing your thoughts.

The Rider – Clinician Relationship in Horsemanship

With guest contributor Kimberly Bench

(www.Benchmark_Farm.com)

This is the third in a series of essays on how we as owners interact with the different professionals that we rely on in the horse world.

The rider – clinician relationship is different from that of a rider and riding instructor. Often, the relationship with the clinician occurs only once or infrequently. The rider – riding instructor relationship is one built for the long term with goals and objectives.

The importance of the clinician/owner relationship: How it complements the owner/trainer relationship

Many riders have successful careers by taking weekly lessons, formulating plans with an instructor, and following through on those plans. Other riders learn from multiple/different instructors and/or a clinician(s) visiting the area that can provide an opportunity for additional learning. For some riders, learning from a trusted trainer and clinician is the optimal combination.

It is important that you take the time to evaluate different clinicians and choose those who will challenge you as a rider, teach you something new, or help you overcome an issue with your horse. If you are working routinely with an instructor, discuss with him/her why you feel that you will benefit from attending the clinic.

Kimberly Bench describes in detail how her farm operates with respect to continuing education and advising students on clinicians:

At our farm, continuing education is a big focus so I try to provide outside educational opportunities for both my students and myself regularly. Last year we had an FEI coach/rider come in monthly – this spring we are lucky enough to be hosting her as a guest instructor for weekly lessons.

I pick clinicians that will compliment my program and enhance what my students are learning at home. Continuity is important, especially in newer/less-experienced riders. I try to go be as involved as possible with my students' education, and I find that attending clinics with them not only allows me the opportunity to learn as well, but also helps me further explain and reinforce the material at home. I will also often speak with the clinician about "homework" for my student after the clinic, which helps make the clinic beneficial to the rider longer term. More seasoned riders may feel confident trying many different clinicians who will offer them a broader perspective, but I find that often times the newer rider is overwhelmed and confused by too many different approaches when it comes very early in their education. It is a great benefit to the rider if the at home instructor attends the clinic with the student, either as a participant or as an auditor.

It is also a good idea to observe (audit) a clinician before participating as a rider. Often times a clinic sounds good but when you get there, you realize the ideas presented are completely contrary to what you believe or perhaps the instructor has a teaching style not suited for your learning abilities. It also gives you the opportunity to be introduced to the material and have a little time to prepare yourself mentally for what you may learn. See how the clinician interacts with the students, the auditors. Is he/she willing to get the horses? Does his teaching approach compliment your existing educational program, your goals? Is the clinician open to questions about why they want you to do something and is he/she willing to break it down if you need further explanation? Is she patient? Does he work well with all levels of riders or is he better with specific groups?

Dr. Mike says, "As an instructor, I encourage my students to attend clinics with other clinicians a few times a year. This helps my riders grow in experience and reinforce or deepen what they are learning at home. After a student attends a clinic, we speak about what he or she learned and how it applies to what is happening on our regular lessons."

One of the benefits of the rider – clinician relationship is that the rider gets to hear the clinician discuss principles and concepts being spoken about and taught by the regular riding instructor. There is a true harmony between the clinician and riding instructor if the clinician is chosen wisely. As is often said "There are many roads to Rome" but you need to find professional horsemen and horsewomen who will compliment your goals. A clinician may do things differently or discuss something from a different perspective but it is important that it make sense with respect to what you are doing with your horse.

For example, Kimberly Bench recently attended a clinic that presented some material that contradicted what she believes about classical riding. Several of the horses became increasingly tense and resistant during their sessions. Kimberly determined that some of this clinician's techniques may have worked for certain horses and riders, but overall it was not an approach she would adopt in her own training/teaching. She was, however, still able to find some valuable insight and a few good idea's to take home, reinforcing the idea that everyone can teach you something – sometimes it's what not to do – but even that has merit!

Both Dr. Mike and Kimberly want to share a moral of this story. As professionals, we often attend a variety of clinics and can find something to learn from the experience. New and less-experienced riders can be caught up in something that doesn't/won't work for them but can't get past the "but I saw it at this clinic and..." Having an educated professional with you at your clinic can help you sort through all of the information and incorporate what is appropriate for you, your horse, and your goals.

Dr. Mike says, "As a clinician I present in areas I have never visited and have no connection to any of the riders or trainers in that location. Because of this, it is very critical that I spend time on the phone or on email with riders or auditors so that I can share my philosophy and approach and let them know the goals of the clinic. I also welcome, at no cost, local instructors to audit my clinics. I want the local trainers, many of whom might have a student attending my clinic, see what I am doing, and ask me questions — it enhances the learning for all. My Dr. Mike's Horsemanship series highlights what I teach and these books, along with my website and essays help people understand who I am as a clinician. It is also important to ask EVERY student throughout the day — "Do you follow what I am teaching?"

How to be a successful rider in a clinic: Preparation and how to be active and learn there

Be prepared for the time commitment of a clinic. You and your horse both need to be physically able to take part in whatever clinic format (discussed later) you have chosen to attend. You and the horse must be up to the demands of more difficult work, therefore, if you have serious goals, you must dedicate the time necessary to reach the level of fitness required to reach those goals in the clinic.

Talk to the clinician about the warm up policy. Some clinicians like to observe the horse and rider in warm up because it can give valuable insight to the horse and rider relationship. Other times a clinician may expect that you have already warmed up and are ready to work so it is important to discuss this with your clinician or clinic organizer before the start of the clinic. Also, ask if you will be allowed into the ring for your warm-up while the rider before you is finishing up. (If you need to lunge your horse also ask about opportunities to do that.)

For your attendance at the clinic, minimize the number of distractions during your lesson time. When you cannot pay full attention to the lesson, you and your horse are not optimally prepared for learning. Distractions can keep you from focusing on the task and this leads to a situation where you or the horse can get hurt. Also consider the other riders – bringing young children, pets, or other distractions may not only distract you, but the clinician, horses and other riders as well.

Make sure you take the time to email or communicate with the clinician or his/her team about your background and goals. A good clinician should be able to help you grow as a rider and push you to excel and you need to accept or discuss with them how much they might be pushing you. Be honest with yourself as well as the clinician as to your level of commitment to reach those goals.

Clinic formats and how to decide what works best for you.

Multiple clinic formats exist and are utilized throughout the US and the rest of the world. We will discuss three formats most commonly encountered.

In every clinic, regardless of the format, it is important for the clinician to adapt to the needs of each rider on that particular day.

As Kimberly Bench said:

The clinic plan needs to be flexible. I always have a rough idea of what I'd like to work on, however, I have to work with what is in front of me that day. Perhaps the horse is a little distracted because snow is sliding off the arena roof. Maybe the rider had a tough workout at the gym and has a stiff back and is having difficulty sitting the trot. A few weeks ago I taught a clinic; one of the riders had emailed me in advance to tell me she wanted to improve her horse's connection at the canter. I believe she thought we would spend the lesson in the canter after the warm up. What I found when I began the lesson was that the horse was not forward and therefore was behind the bit and on the forehand. He was also dull to her leg aides. We went back to the basics of sending the horse forward into the contact, we worked on leg yielding in and out on a circle and then on a parallel line. I also adjusted her position as the way she was sitting had her seat bones facing backwards, restricting the horses desire to swing through in the back. The majority of the lesson was spent in the walk and trot. However, near the end of the lesson when I asked them to canter again the connection problem had resolved.

If I had restricted myself to a detailed lesson plan, we could have spent 45 minutes of cantering poorly. Cantering itself does not improve cantering, just as asking for 100 flying changes does not fix a problem with the flying change. It is my job to identify what issues need to be addressed; guide the horse and rider through exercises that help improve the work and instruct them on how to achieve the desired results. It is also my job to help the rider understand the bigger picture and strict lesson plans are often detrimental to the overall goal.

Similar experiences have been encountered by Dr. Mike who says, "It is the job of the clinician to adjust and adapt to accommodate each student's learning style and to help make sure a strong foundation exists. Once that foundation exists and is the basis for good fundamentals, many problems are solved."

Format #1 — Multiple riders over a single day or multiple days — the group option

In the group format, anywhere from 5 to 30 riders may attend a clinic and take instruction. For some people this works well because they have frequent break periods while the clinician is working with someone else on a particular issue. Also, for some people, learning is easier when they see everything done by someone else and can process what they are learning simultaneously. This type of clinic may run 1 to 4 days and can be a lot to take in for some riders and horses.

Format #2 — Riders scheduled one at a time with auditors — the one-on-one option

With private sessions, one on one time is set and the clinician works with riders independently. Other riders and auditors may watch and learn. Often times the clinician will stop and ask if the auditors have any questions about what was covered in between riders. This format allows the clinician to give more focused feedback and works well for rider who want a more detailed, intense lesson.

Format #3 — Group lesson in the morning and then private sessions with each rider in the afternoon

This format can provide the benefits of the two previously mentioned formats where the group session introduces the concepts and then the individual sessions can fine tune the application of them.

In summary:

1) Find a clinic and clinician that will help you move forward with your goals. Make sure the clinic format works for you and that you and your riding instructor (if applicable) have discussed the right clinician for you.

2) Be prepared to learn. By this you need to be physically fit, not distracted, and devoted to the learning opportunity.

3) As always — have fun and practice safe horsemanship.

Kimberly Bench, co-author of this essay, is a clinician, instructor and horsewoman specializing in Classical Dressage. She owns and operates Benchmark Farm in Hudsonville, MI. She has developed a program she calls "Practical Dressage" which is designed to teach riders of any discipline how the classical training scale can work for them. Find more information at:

http://www.Benchmark-Farm.com

The Horse Owner - Veterinarian/Farrier/Chiropractor/ Body Worker-Massager Relationship

The Horse Owner's relationship with the Veterinarian/Farrier/Chiropractor/Body Worker-Massager is critical for the health and well-being of your horse. Thirty or forty years ago, this relationship included the Veterinarian and Farrier with very few people using Equine Chiropractic or Body Worker-Massage. In recent times, the health care team for your horse has expanded to include chiropractors and body worker-massage practitioners yet the basics of the relationship remain the same.

1) Most important of all is that your horse needs to be prepared for treatment by these professionals.

As an owner, you need to either train your horse or have a trainer work with you and/or your horse to help your horse behave correctly for these professionals. This is very important for the safety of your horse, your equine health care provider, and you.

So what is needed -- your horse needs to be able to be caught easily, stand still (at least stand mostly still and quiet), be touched all over the body, and pick up his/her feet with ease. These professionals are not hired to train your horse; they are employed to provide health care. If your horse is difficult for you to handle, have a trainer or other qualified equine professional there to assist these people.

2) Both the owner and the equine health care professional need to be respectful of each others time.

If either is going to be late, notify the other person. If you need to change the appointment, do so as soon as possible.

3) Develop a relationship -- this goes both ways.

Understand what services the health care professional provides and what he/she is willing to do for you and your horse. The health care providers also need to understand what the owner is seeking in a health care professional and if this is not something they want to provide, recommend another colleague for the job.

4) Respect the knowledge of the health care provider - but always ask for clarification.

As an owner, once you have selected a professional, trust him or her to do the job correctly but make sure you are satisfied with the answers and the continual care of your horse. There may be a time that you do not understand or think what is being done is correct -- immediately ask for more information because you as the owner need to make informed decisions. If you decide the health care provider is no longer doing what is best for your horse, select another caregiver. If you want a second opinion, tell the health care provider you will be seeking a second opinion and tell him/her why. Often times, especially with lameness, it is a good idea to get a second look but be open about it with the health care provider.

5) Ask for an estimate of charges, anticipated outcomes, and approximation of time involved.

Nothing ruins a relationship with your equine health care provider than surprises in the amount being charged. Your health care provider should be able to give you an estimate on routine work and be pretty close to that estimate. Often, you must ask for estimated costs, frequency of necessary treatments, and expected outcomes. Nothing is ever guaranteed in health care but anticipated outcomes can be discussed. The amount of time to complete a treatment or achieve healing can be estimated but exceptions do occur.

6) Follow the treatment instructions.

If you are given a prescribed treatment, make sure you follow the instructions because this will help in keeping the treatment/healing process on time.

7) Know who your equine health care provider recommends in the event that he/she is out of town or unable to assist you.

Ask them who takes their calls when they are away and how best you can get hold of the person who will provide temporary care. This is important, especially for emergency medical situations. You do not need to be surprised and have to pull out the yellow pages to find a veterinarian who will assist you. Most often equine practitioners have their answering service refer you to another available veterinarian.

Thinking about these seven items can help you to build a successful relationship with your Veterinarian/Farrier/Chiropractor/Body Worker-Massager.

The Horse Owner – Stable/Arena Owner/Manager Relationship

For those who do not have the opportunity to stable a horse at home, the boarding facility is critical for the care and well-being of our horses. Many times for shows or events, we ride at an arena and have to work with facility managers. By following these guidelines, you can establish a very positive relationship with your Stable/Arena owner/manager.

Boarding Facility Relationship

1) Understand and follow the rules of the boarding facility. Those rules are in place for safety of you and your horse and for other stable occupants. One of the rules is likely to tell you when board payments are due each month. Be on time or speak to the facility manager if there is an issue. Do not make them chase you down for your board bill. If you are trading help around the facility for a reduction in your board costs, make sure to do the work you have committed to for the facility.

2) Appreciate that many times the facility is also home to the family/person that runs the boarding stable so it is important to respect their private spaces/homes.

3) Be respectful of common equipment. If manure carts and rakes are available for all to use, replace them in the appropriate place after each use.

4) Take care to show consideration for other boarders, their equipment, and their horses. It is nice to be helpful but do not be intrusive. If the person you are trying to help does not seem to want your assistance, then leave them alone.

5) Clean up after yourself both in the arena and around the facility.

6) Keep your personal contact information up to date with the facility manager so that you can be contacted easily if your horse is in need of attention.

7) If you bring your children to the facility, make sure they stay out of harm's way and are not disruptive to other boarders or horses.

8) If the facility manager offers to help you by taking care of your horse during veterinary, furrier, chiropractor, or massage/body-worker visits, make sure that the health care professional and the facility manger both know exactly what you want done and that you are reachable by phone during the appointment.

Riding Arena Relationship

1) Understand and follow the rules of the riding arena. Those rules are in place for safety of you and your horse and for other stable occupants. Know where you can tie up your horse and know if you can lunge or do other work with your horse in the arena.

2) Take care to show consideration for other riders in and around the arena.

3) Clean up after yourself around the facility.

4) Park only in designated parking areas.

5) Make sure that as you drive through the facility you are watching out for riders, horses, and pedestrians.

6) Sign the release of liability that all facilities need to have on file to allow you to participate in events.

CHAPTER 4

Essays on Leadership
In Horsemanship

In this four part series, I will be exploring my Leadership in Horsemanship philosophy. The four components to my leadership philosophy include:

i. Honesty

ii. Wholeness

iii. Creativity

iv. Safety

Part I
Honesty

Part I is a discussion about the Honesty component. Honesty as part of our Leadership in Horsemanship can be thought of from two perspectives. First — are we honest with our own self and secondly — are we honest with our horse.

Honesty with self

Being honest with ourselves is important in setting and achieving goals. Honesty is part of our moral character and refers to positive, virtuous attributes including integrity, truthfulness, and straightforwardness.

As we work to be the leader for our horse(s), we need to look at ourselves and perform an assessment of our physical, emotional, and mental capabilities. We also need to assess our financial and time constraints. Finally, we need to honestly assess our abilities as riders and trainers.

We need to honestly determine how much our body can physically handle of the care and maintenance of our horses. This is very difficult because as we age, get ill, or have an injury we are forced to re-evaluate how much we can accomplish. We never want to admit physical weaknesses but in reality, our physical limitations can hurt our horses and that is why we need to be Honest about our physical abilities.

We need to honestly evaluate our emotional and mental abilities. Do we have the ability to give our horses the sense of confidence that comes from inside of us? Are we emotionally and mentally able to take care of the animal?

Now wait a minute you are saying — there are many stories where horses help people gain confidence and I immediately agree with you. Horses can be great inspiration for gaining confidence — if we have the right horse. Nevertheless, the important part is to understand what our role is in that process and the type of horse that can help us achieve greater confidence. We need to honestly assess if the good-natured horse can help us achieve that goal as opposed to the six month old that might run us over.

The financial and time constraints are actually the easiest to assess. Do we have the money (with a 3 to 6 month reserve) to take care of our horses now and in an emergency and do we have the time to feed and care for them each day (or pay a boarding facility to do that part) and do we have the time to spend with them.

True Horsemen and Horsewomen constantly assess their abilities as riders and trainers. These people can tell you what they can and cannot do. By knowing and acknowledging what you can and cannot do at this moment in time, it will better help you develop your goals — something that is part of Wholeness. Therefore, for each person, this self-assessment is so important because it helps us with Part II — Wholeness. However, before we get to part II, we need to think about our honesty with horses.

Honesty with the horse

Honesty with horses comes down to the concept of "straightforwardness." Are we direct and truthful with our horses?

Let me share with you two examples of working with horses and then choose the one that exhibits honesty.

Example #1 — John goes out to the barn. He has his earphones in, talking on his phone. His horse walks into the stall and John ignores the horse as he gets his saddle out and collects his spurs all the while talking on the phone. The horse walks out of the stall. John gets the halter, walks out to the pen, and calls the horse to him. The horse walks over to John and the halter is put on. John is still talking on his cell phone and walks to the stall. John ties the horse up and then pushes his butt over with a shove. The horse is saddled; John gets on and rides, while still talking on his cell phone. The horse is twitching his ears trying to understand what John wants (John is to busy talking to be reading any of the horse's body language). John tells his phone companion that the horse is pissy and that he is going to hang up now since this horse needs to lope some circles to get respect.

Example #2 — Judy goes out to the barn. She has her earphones in, talking on the phone. As she gets to the barn, she hangs up from the call and puts her cell phone away. Her horse walks into the stall and Judy says hi and then gets his saddle out and collects her spurs. Judy gets the halter, the horse easily puts his head into the halter, and Judy finishes the haltering and ties the horse up. Judy gives the horse a pre-signal and aide to move his butt over and the horse immediately complies. The horse is saddled; Judy walks him out a few steps and asks the horse to give to pressure. Judy mounts and goes out for a good ride.

Both stories end in a ride on the horse — but example #2 is a person who is honest with the horse. Judy gives clear direction and is straightforward with her intent. She comes to the barn and is engaged and active about riding her horse. Example #1 is full of misdirection, confusion and lies because John is trying to ride and talk on the phone and not giving pre-signals or clear guidance to the horse.

Which of the two riders would you want to accept as your leader?

Conclusion

Be honest with yourself and what you can actually do and treat your horse with directness (straightforwardness) and you will find that your horse is more willing to accept you as his/her leader.

Part II
Wholeness

Part II continues with some ideas around the concept of Wholeness. Webster's Online Dictionary defines *Wholeness* as "An undivided or unbroken completeness or totality with nothing wanting." That certainly seems to be a mouthful but as I read that definition it struck me that it defines what we are all seeking with horses. How cool!

I fixated on the words "nothing wanting" and have contemplated how this fits in with leadership and it struck me that one of the keys of Leadership in Horsemanship is being able to put together a complete package that includes, horse, and rider working as a team.

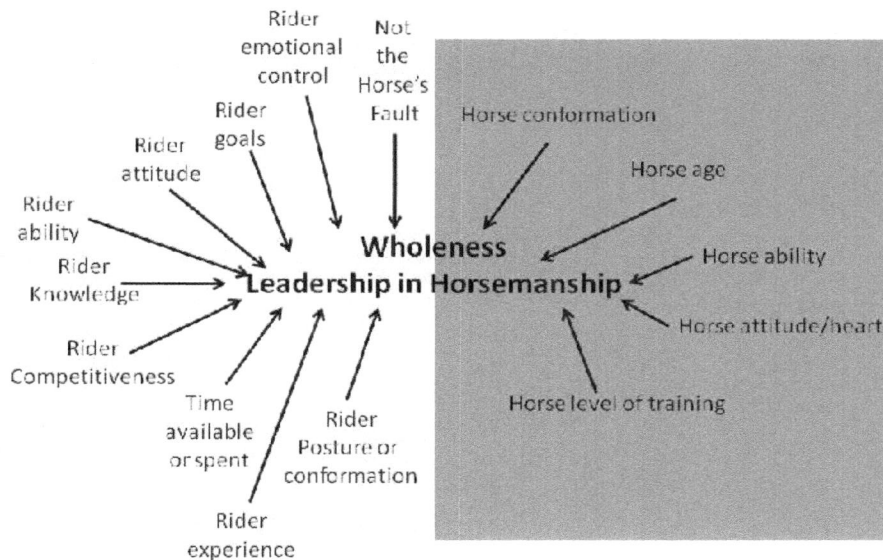

Rider emotional control

Not the Horse's Fault

Horse conformation

Rider goals

Horse age

Rider attitude

Rider ability

Horse ability

Rider Knowledge

Wholeness
Leadership in Horsemanship

Horse attitude/heart

Rider Competitiveness

Time available or spent

Rider Posture or conformation

Horse level of training

Rider experience

In Wholeness, we seek to understand how everything fits together. The best way I could represent this concept is in the form of a figure with many of the components that make up the complete package of horse and rider. I may be missing some components and I always encourage you to share your ideas and comment.

One of many things worth noting in this diagram is that I shaded those items that the horse brings. Notice how the horse brings five items whereas the human brings so many more. The sum of all makes the complete/whole package a success.

Conclusion

As we take into account the honesty portion and now add wholeness, we see how much of the equation for leadership in horses relies on the human component. To work on our leadership, we need to constantly evaluate where we are with each of the human components and assess our horse on his/her part of this matrix.

Part III
Creativity

We are half way through the four components of leadership so it is appropriate to recap. Part I is Honesty. In honesty, we need to analyze what we can and cannot do at any given time. Sometimes we are not ready for the challenge presented by a horse — but we can learn and get ready. We also need to be straightforward in our dealings with the horses we are working with. Part II described an analysis of the Whole situation — Wholeness. In Wholeness, we need to understand how our actions and those of the horse create reactions.

Part III deals with Creativity in leadership. Every good leader will admit that he/she do not always have the answer. A leader is someone who gathers information and adapts to changes. So you ask — how does Creativity apply to leadership with horses.

Well as leaders of horses, we need to adapt our methods and approaches to work with each and every horse. Horses are unique and as long as we use principles such as "Pressure and Release", "Foundation training activities" and understand the "Prey vs. Predator" relationship, we should be able to find/create new ways to work with each and every horse.

While we all know that repetition and consistency help in training, we also need to make sure we are creative and keeping the horse thinking and responding to our aides and signals rather than anticipating what we want.

Here are some examples of how we can employ creativity in our horsemanship leadership:

1) Learn new methods from other people

2) Adapt/change an old method to work safely in the current situation

3) Use different exercises to help teach your horse a specific task

4) Use cross-training when teaching your horse

5) Attend a clinic being taught for a different discipline

6) Take a lesson with a new instructor

7) Ride a new horse that can teach you

Overall, Creativity in Leadership for Horsemanship focuses on the human person learning multiple ways to teach a horse something. There may be 10 safe ways to teach a horse something new — we should be creative (not boring) and learn how to apply those ten different ways.

One of the ways I continually work to be creative is that I get to work with other trainers and I also attend (as a participant) clinics taught by others. What I want to emphasize here is that for you to be the leader for your horse and to develop strong teamwork and success — you need to develop a relationship that is full of new experiences. Teach your horse something new, but expose them to many different, creative, and new ways that you may ask them to perform.

Part IV
Safety

Although last in the discussion, safety is likely the most important component of Leadership for Horsemanship. Think back to a time, possibly in college or high school, where somebody asked you to be part of something wild and crazy and it turned out to be unsafe. If we are honest with ourselves, we need to admit that when someone puts us in an unsafe situation we begin to trust him or her less and less. In fact, we may distance ourselves from someone who is not safe.

Now let us think about safety in terms of our horsemanship and being a leader. If you never practice safety with your horse and your horse continually gets into predicaments/hurt/scared because of your lack of safety — it is very probable that your horse will not look to you for leadership.

A while back, I was touching base with a fellow horsemanship coach (Kristina Mundy); she said something that is spot on accurate. Kristina said "…owners must be dedicated to the good of their horse…" and I would add that the good of the horse means the safety of the horse.

So let us ask a series of questions to evaluate how safe we are with our horses:

1) Do we check our tack each time to make sure it is ready for the ride?

2) Do we scout the trail or get info from someone who has ridden the same path?

3) Do we use proper equipment for protection of our horse (leg wraps, shoes/proper trims, etc.)

4) Do we ride with a helmet?

5) Do we pay attention and ride actively so that we see potential issues before they can hurt us?

6) Do we ride with safe people?

7) Is our hauling equipment (trailer, truck, etc) safe to operate?

8) Do we check our horse out for 1 to 2 minutes of groundwork before riding?

9) Do we wear appropriate clothing and footwear when working with horses?

Therefore, when we speak of safety there is an underlying debate out there. Some folks say — I have ridden for years and never needed to pay attention to any of those things. Others are concerned about the relationship and protection of their horses so they consider each one of the above questions. Those that consider safety first are sometimes silently laughed at by those who have "ridden a long time and never been hurt."

Two final points about safety as part of Leadership for Horsemanship.

1) If you practice safety first, then you significantly decrease the chance of you and your horse getting hurt. If you are not hurt, then you should be mentally and physically able to help your horse. If you get hurt — who is going to help your horse? I sure would want a leader who can help me if I get into a bad spot…and I am certain your horse wants a leader who can keep him/her safe.

Now it is this second point that I know has the biggest area of disagreement but I want to make sure I say a few words here.

2) <u>Children under the age of 18 should wear a helmet while riding.</u> Why under the age of 18 — because after that you are an adult and can make your own choices. If we want to see the next generation of great equestrians — we need to help them be safe. There should be no need for laws…this should be common sense. (Note: my equine liability insurance requires that all students under the age of 18 wear a helmet while I am teaching)

The Centers for Disease Control (CDC) cite some interesting statistics relating to Traumatic Brain Injury (TBI) and horseback riding with respect to children. Click here for information:

cdc.gov/mmwr/preview/mmwrhtml/mm6039a1.htm

In a nutshell — the above CDC link will share with you the following information:

During 2001–2009, an estimated 2,651,581 children aged ≤19 years were treated annually for sports and recreation–related injuries. Approximately 6.5%, or 173,285 of these injuries, were TBIs. Overall, the activities associated with the greatest estimated number of TBI-related Emergency Department (ED) visits were bicycling, football, playground activities, basketball, and soccer. <u>Activities for which TBI accounted for >10% of the injury ED visits for that activity included horseback riding (15.3%) [this is ~2900 kids per year]</u>, ice skating (11.4%), golfing (11.0%), all-terrain vehicle riding (10.6%), and tobogganing/sledding (10.2%). One more link with information worth reading is found here:

biak.us/brain-injury-and-horses

I encourage all of you with children to have them wear helmets and I urge all of us to speak to our delegates from the different breed associations, rodeo events, 4H, FFA and other horsemanship activities to find ways to encourage children to wear helmets.

In summary — practice being safe. To be that leader that your horse wants, you need to be healthy and able to help your horse. If you become injured — who is going to take care of your horse partner?

CHAPTER 5

On the Trail
Trail Guide

Be <u>AWARE</u> on the trail

<u>Ac</u>quaint yourself with the trail and the area where you are riding

<u>Wa</u>tch the trail/weather for unsafe and changing conditions

<u>Ac</u>tively ride your horse, do not just be a passenger

<u>Re</u>spect other riders/bikers/hikers on the trail

<u>En</u>joy the ride

General comments on this Guide

As I developed the 6 C's of horsemanship, I made sure these ideas work for riding in the arena, on the trail and in competition. When we ride, we want to be confident in our riding skills and our horse. How do we gain confidence---we practice, learn from others, go to clinics and we take small steps. If I wanted to ride on a 5-day trail ride, I would first build up my confidence and my horse's confidence by taking a 1-day ride. In order for us to gain confidence, we need to learn to control our horse and the space around our horse. To build confidence and establish control we need to practice with ---- consistency.

As a rider, it is our obligation to be consistent in our training and riding methods. When we are consistent, have a plan, and follow our plan we build confidence in our horse and our abilities. To maintain control we need to keep our bodies and our horse's body ---- collected. We cannot expect control when our arms are waving all around and our horses are racing through open fields.

Maintaining collection of our body, our speed and the horse's flexibility helps us to be confident and in control. As we teach our horse, we need to remember to have ---- compassion. When I go out on a trail ride I want to enjoy time with my horse and I want to enjoy the scenery and most of all I want this to be full of ---- calmness. As we embark on the day and each time we go to the barn remember---our horse should be just as calm at the end of our ride as he was when he was standing in his stall.

Preparation of the Rider

Clothes
Wear layers and comfortable clothing. Never wear ill-fitting clothing because it will be uncomfortable and make for a less pleasurable ride. Make sure you are carrying a jacket if the weather has a chance to get cool. Plan ahead and have a small rain parka handy if it might rain. Wear a helmet to protect yourself from the elements and for YOUR SAFETY.

Food
Bring snacks to munch on along the trail. If we get hungry, we tend to want to hurry up, we lose patience, and we forget to remain calm and collected.

Water

Drink plenty of water to keep yourself hydrated. Never drink water from small streams or ponds. If you cannot pack enough water for your ride carry along some tablets that you can use to decontaminate the water.

Environmental protections

Wear sunscreen, lip balm, and insect repellent if needed. Protect yourself by keeping the elements from hurting you.

Physical fitness

Have your body ready for the ride. If you are planning a 5-day trail ride, prepare yourself by taking small rides before your long ride. If you have a bad knee or bad ankle, wear a brace. Stretch before you get into the saddle. Loosen yourself up and it will make the ride more comfortable. Stretching exercises, leg lunges, yoga or anything that can help loosen your muscles and joints will help you for a long day in the saddle.

Alert friends and family as to when and where you are going to ride

This is very important and can save your life. If something happens to you on the ride, the search and rescue teams or your family would have an easier time finding you and your horse if they know where you have gone riding. Go on a trail ride with other riders can also help you get assistance should something unfortunate happen.

Preparation of the Horse

Pre-ride maintenance:

Hoof care
Have your horse's feet in good shape before you head out on the trail.

Vaccinations
West Nile Virus vaccine is a must as is the combination shot for tetanus, flu, and encephalitis (Western, Eastern, and Venezuelan). Consult with your veterinarian and establish a proper vaccination strategy that works for you and your horse.

Health certificates
If you are traveling out of state, have a current health certificate (good for 30 days) and Coggins (good for 180 days) for your horse. Your veterinarian can help you get everything order. Always travel with a copy of your horse's registration papers.

Training and fitness for your horse
In the next section, we will discuss foundation-training exercises that will help you improve your confidence as a rider. These exercises also help your horse to be prepared for anything you may want to teach your horse. Some of the exercises are great for helping navigate the trail and for getting past obstacles. Use these exercises to achieve fitness and preparation for longer rides.

Equipment/Tack
Before each ride, you should always inspect your tack and make sure there are no broken stitches, broken buckles, or anything wrong with your tack that might compromise the safety for your horse or yourself. This is something we should always do before riding at home OR on the trail.

I highly recommend using leg protection on all four legs of your horse whenever you ride your horse, especially on the trail. At a minimum, the front legs should have protection.

Water and Feed

Make sure your horse has plenty of opportunities to drink. Learn from other riders where water is available for your horse. If you are staging from a campsite know the rules regarding hay for your horse. You may be required to purchase hay that is certified weed free.

Exercises for better preparing you and the horse for trail riding - On the ground and in the saddle:

I recommend you work with your horse using my *Ground Steps to Success* to help you prepare your horse and yourself for going out on the trail.

Another activity that will help you when you are out on the trail and in new surroundings:

Walking with respect. It has been said by many horsemen and women --- we ride the horse we lead. What does this mean exactly? Well if our horse does not respect us on the ground, crowds us, and pushes us …we can expect the same behavior while we are riding in the saddle. So what can we do to gain the respect of our horse?

Four exercises that will help you gain respect
1) Round pen work
Practice inside and outside turns with your horse, ask for speed control, watch him, and keep him out of your space. Establish respect by getting his attention to your requests and his respect in a safe environment.

2) Go forward cue

Teach your horse to go forward whenever you ask. Simply point your left hand forward, ask your horse to walk forward and tap on his hindquarters if he needs encouragement. Do not stop until your horse goes forward. Make sure you are standing behind the withers as you tap on the rear end to drive the horse forward. Repeat everything from the right side of your horse.

3) Granny walk

Walk in a slow controlled forward motion. This makes your horse focus on what you are asking. When you and your horse walk slower, it gives you both time to think before you act.

4) Go on a long walk with your horse

Walk with your horse and when he crowds you, stop him, and ask him to back up a step. If he walks ahead of you, stop him and make him back up. If he pushes his shoulder into you, make him disengage his hip or move his shoulders over so that his energy is used for something constructive. Do not accept bad behavior. I have listed many tools above that you can use to gain respect of your horse on the ground.

Practice Stopping

One-rein emergency stop. Place hand on the rein and pull gently but firmly towards your knee. Make sure that you are not squeezing with your legs. Exhale and say WHOOOOAAAAA. Practice this from both sides. A hand can be placed on the saddle for stability. If your horse moves his hips over that is entirely okay and will be very helpful in slowing forward motion. Do not release the rein until your horse comes to a complete stop. Please practice this at a standstill, at the walk and at the trot.

PRACTICE PRACTICE PRACTICE

As we, all work to build a relationship with our horses we need to practice. If I work with my horse every day I keep that trust established and I keep his mind focused on me as his leader. We do not always have hours to spend each day but every time we go into his stall/pen, it is an opportunity for us to remind the horse that we work together as a team. 5 minutes of work each day can alleviate problems down the road.

De-Spooking

Many of us have heard horse experts, friends, and family members tell us about the horses natural response to a fearful situation referred to as the "fight or flight response." When most horses are confronted with an uncomfortable situation, they most often choose to distance themselves from this object (that is the flight response). Some horses run away, others snort at the object and slowly move away, some face the object and flare nostrils while others jump all directions and seemingly loose all brain function.

We as riders and owners most certainly do not enjoy these situations and our own fears and survival mechanisms rise up to protect us. Each of us is on a journey to be safe when riding. Some people look to develop that "bomb-proof" horse. What exactly defines a "bomb-proof" horse is still a topic of discussion. For some people they want a horse that will never move a muscle when confronted with something new. Others want a horse that will simply become more alert but not immediately go into a flight mode.

4 Part Harmony for De-spooking

1 part emotional control
1 part trust
1 part wisdom/understanding
1 part "time"

Emotional control + Trust + Wisdom/Understanding + Time

The above equation is an easy way of remembering everything we need for helping our horse get over fear of something. We do not need special equipment.

First, we need emotional control. It is NEVER NEVER NEVER the horse's fault therefore; we cannot get mad at the horse. Most horses when confronted with a "spooky" object will have a raised emotional level and be excited. We as the rider need to accept that this will happen and then we proceed with the training and never blame the horse. Never blame the breed, sex, or age of the horse. We stay calm and we stay focused on achieving our objective---to de-sensitize our horse to the "spooky" object.

Secondly, we need to establish a relationship of trust with our horse. If our horse has trust in us then de-spooking will be much easier to accomplish. I said easier --- not simple and with no work. How do we develop trust? We work with our horse and teach our horse to look to us as the leader.

The third part is wisdom and understanding. We as the rider need to develop a knowledge base and learn how to de-spook a horse, how to interpret a horse's actions, how to plan a series of activities and exercises that will help us "de-spook" our horse. We need to understand that a horse is a fight or flight animal and >90% will choose to run away if given the opportunity. Understand this and work with your horse. Have the understanding and wisdom that 1 day of work will not solve all your problems and give you a perfectly de-spooked horse.

Finally, but most importantly, this process takes time. If you want that horse that does not run away from new objects then you need to spend the time to work with your horse. How long will it take--- this depends on each rider and each horse because both are unique. Some may be de-spooked in 5 minutes; others might need 5 months.

If we work on not getting agitated and maintain our emotions, then we can develop a trusting relationship with our horse. Add in some wisdom and understanding and lots of time and you are on the road to success.

Safety practices when you are working with your horse in a spooky situation

1) Wear a helmet.

2) Other riders MUST pay attention and step away to provide the spooky horse with 10-20 feet of clear space (NO RUBBER-NECKING).

3) Stop and think a moment about how to handle the training your horse will need to help them be de-spooked (do not react with your emotions).

4) Practice the four-part harmony I described above.

5) TAKE PLENTY OF TIME.

6) Do not be afraid to get off and be on the ground rather than in the saddle.

7) Remember to stop and breathe after you have made an accomplishment. Let your horse think every so often rather than force them to continue to react.

Other Books by Michael Guerini

NON-FICTION

Dr. Mike's Horsemanship Ground Steps to Success

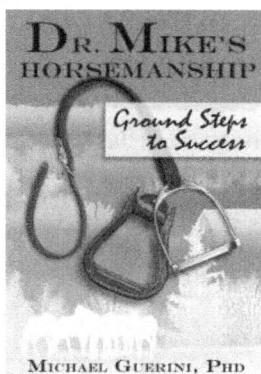

Ground Steps to Success includes: 1) Preparation for Ground work and Riding 2) Understanding your Horse's body language 3) Pre-signal and preparatory commands, and 4) Ground Steps to Success (walk, whoa, disengage hips, back, go forward cue and other movements). This book is great for improving the foundation training basics and building a better horse.

Dr. Mike's Horsemanship Responsive Riding for Advanced Horsemanship

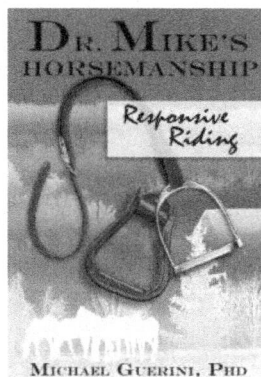

In this book, Dr. Mike provides numerous training exercises so that riders will gain a better feel of the horse. Each exercise is well described and shares with you the benefit of performing the exercise. The book includes multiple warm-up exercises (ex. riding with straightness, trotting on the oval, etc.) for getting better directional control and the proper use of your legs when riding. Advanced exercises (ex. Staircase leg yields, 10-10-10 exercise, etc) are included for enhanced responsiveness. The basics of dressage and proper biomechanics are presented to help you improve your body language and pre-signal communications with your horse.

NON-FICTION

Dr. Mike's Horsemanship Riding Exercises

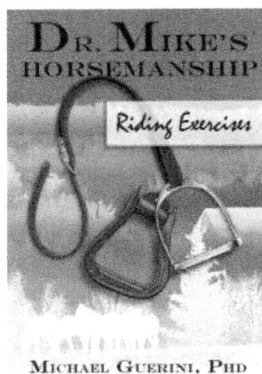

This book includes 12 easy to follow riding exercises complete with written instructions and diagrams. Great for warm-ups and giving you and your horse some new challenges. These exercises incorporate Classical and Western Dressage Elements and are great for Horsemanship patterns.

Dr. Mike's Horsemanship Horse Owners Modern Keys for Success

A collection of Essays from many years of successful horsemanship. This book focuses on ideas to help new horse owners build a strong foundation of thoughts and ideas for success in owning, riding, and training horses.

Available in print and digital formats

FICTION

Old Towne: Beginnings

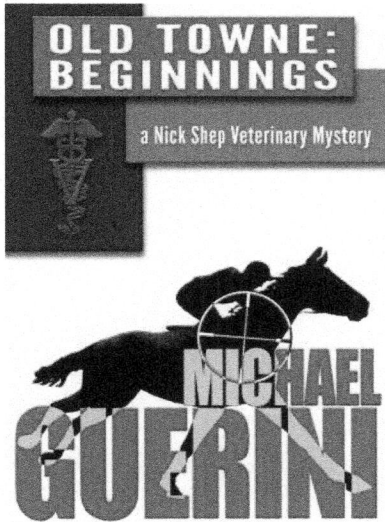

The worlds of veterinary medicine and biotechnology collide in this fictional account of Dr. Shep, a former biotechnology scientist who now works as a veterinarian. In Old Towne: Beginnings, Dr. Shep embarks on a new path in his career and at the same time, he must solve a mystery concerning a sick horse and a devious plan by others to make money. Along the way, he introduces you to his team (Misty and Scott) and a variety of animals that he treats and helps

Of Horses & Life

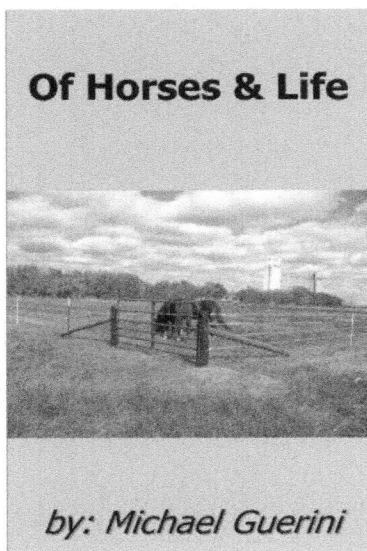

A collection of 10 poems about life with horses. The poems are entitled: Baby Horse; Cowhorse; Young Rider's First Lesson; My New Owner; Big Bad Cuttin Horse; Show Jumping; Horse Girl; A Visit from the Farrier; Feeding Time at the Barn and Old Horse.

Made in the USA
Las Vegas, NV
09 February 2022